Soul Priority

A True Story of the Soul's Journey from
Death to Rebirth and
The Four Soul Archetypes that Activate
Your Soul Assignment

———————————————

By Mariko Frederick

D1715856

Soul Priority: A True Story of the Soul's Journey from Death to Rebirth and The Four Soul Archetypes that Activate Your Soul Assignment

CONTENTS

Dedication

For my daughter Hema. It was always you.

Introduction

My sincerest wish is that this book serves as a bridge from your soul to your daily life.

Please read with a heart as open as your eyes because your view of life will expand and lead you to make discoveries about your life as you'll see that it did in mine. It is natural for people to be hesitant to speak about life's deep layers of energy, and my aim in writing this book is to make conversations about the human spirit happen with ease and grace.

PART I:
Remember Who You Are

Chapter 1

Death: Witnessed and Experienced

I had seen death, but never witnessed it so clearly before that moment. Medical personnel in Intensive Care Units (ICUs) provide acute care to very sick or injured people with the intention of saving their lives. There, facing down death is met with a monumental fight by nurses, doctors, respiratory therapists, and other technicians.

At the age of 29 I had become comfortable witnessing both peaceful deaths and fights for life that sometimes ended in death. Those experiences led to my intense interest in living and filling my life with as much rock climbing, hiking, backpacking, and meditation as I could fit in.

Happy, healthy, newly married, I left my life in the ICU and felt at home practicing alternative medicine.

I thought the universe had guided me to be the person I was meant to be—that I had arrived at the pinnacle of adulthood.

My years in the ICU, followed by my extraordinary path into practicing in Chinese medicine, validated that this was the life I was meant to live.

Knowing who I was and what I was meant to do let me live with a deep satisfaction. Nothing could derail me from my path—because after all—it was meant to be.

And then I died.

On the day I died, I was home, in bed, feeling the heaviness of my body, as if I were made entirely of iron. I couldn't move anything, and everything hurt so much—I felt a raking, sharp pain throughout my entire body.

I couldn't even call out to my husband Chris for help. All I could do was lay there, helpless, and feel the life force drain from my body. Was I extremely tired? Sick? I didn't know what was happening, but I assumed I would recover.

Despite all I knew about Chinese medicine—after six years in practice by then—I could do nothing to help myself. The strange thing is, I wasn't worried.

Although I recognized the life force draining out of me as water can drain out of a pool, I never once had the feeling or thought, "I'm dying."

As more and more of my life force withdrew, I automatically began to focus solely on breathing. I felt my breath rise and fall until all awareness rested in my lungs. That part of my body felt so heavy—like an enormous iron weight was crushing me. Each inhalation took an immense effort. It felt like an eternity of just pushing the iron weight up and letting it fall back down.

"Breathing is really overrated," I thought as I was inhaling and pushing that weight back up…letting it fall…pushing it up…letting it fall…pushing it back up…until..."I think I'll stop."

Everything went still. There was no sound from my breath or my heart—only a faint buzz from my nervous system. I hadn't known my nervous system made any sound until that final moment when I heard it quietly drift away. Somewhere, a tiny part of me recognized that by not continuing to breathe I would die. Yet, in that same moment I felt more alive than I had during those previous moments of working so hard to breathe.

"Ah, that's better," I thought. "Breathing's so unnecessary. It's funny we think we have to do it."

The pain disappeared. I no longer felt drained. My gaze was fixed at the point between my eyebrows—what's known as the spiritual eye. But I was not just focused there—I was locked into place as if nothing else existed—just that point.

My spiritual eye was lit up like a thousand suns shining directly at me—into me. The light felt familiar as if it had always been there, only I had forgotten about it. I took comfort from it.

The next thing I knew, I floated above the bedroom, and was watching Chris in the kitchen as he was preparing tea for me. "He'll be all right. He'll remarry. It won't be the same, but he'll be OK. I just wish I had given him a child." I could feel in my heart the scenario in which my husband's life would continue; his new marriage, and a child. It was definitely not the same depth of love we'd shared but I knew he'd be all right. My heart welled with an immense love and appreciation for Chris, my parents, my sister, and even our wolf dog, Bodhi. I wasn't leaving them, just stepping through to the other side of a thin veil. The love that tied us together remained.

Chapter 2

Behind the Veil

I was no longer in our house but in another place that I couldn't see with my human eyes—the vision I had become accustomed to. Yet I could see clearly. The "place" I was in was void of any light yet, somehow, not dark. It felt so peaceful that even a single ray of light would've been foreign. It felt like it was expanding infinitely in all directions, like being in outer space without lights from fiery planets in the galaxies. I was experiencing infinite space made from the vibration of peace.

I became aware of the unending and unconditional love of our Divine Creator. I knew I was on my way Home. I wasn't alone though. The loving Soul that guided me here let me know that I was to go through a process—my life review.

This felt natural; expected. The Soul that guided me wasn't someone I felt I knew, not a friend or family member, but rather a Divine Being performing its job to usher souls through this process.

I never once felt afraid—I only felt unconditional love.

My life review began. It seemed like watching a movie of my own life—just the most important parts. Mundane things, like each time I brushed my teeth or tied my shoes, were skipped. I only experienced the moments of decision and interaction. Each mistake I made, each bad decision, each time I hurt someone's feelings, each time I ignored my intuition, each time I loved someone, each encouraging or compassionate word I gave someone, each person I ever helped—it was all there—everything that really mattered. This movie felt interactive, and I was able to experience my life one more time.

Much of my review from birth to becoming a toddler was filled with love.

The real lessons began at 5 years old when I made my first big mistake. It was when I had my friend Sherri over to play for the first time. We walked by the fence line between my house and our neighbor's house under their large shade tree. Her little fingers pointed at something on the ground, and she let out a giggle. Large paw prints had been pressed into fresh cement with a name etched under it. I said, "That's Tiger. He's dead."

I watched her smile turn into shock and I felt her remorse and asked, "How would you like it if you died and everyone laughed? What if no one missed you?" I went on to say, "The people who owned this dog are probably crying and you're laughing at them." On and on I went, ruthlessly scolding her. Yet, all the while, I was feeling how much I was hurting her. When she cried, I finally stopped attacking her with my words. Not because I cared, but because I didn't want to get into trouble for lying. I had no idea if Tiger had died or not. I wanted to be mean and hurt her on purpose.

In my life review I experienced my actions from Sherri's point of view. I saw myself through her eyes and felt firsthand the emotional pain I'd caused. I now felt as if Sherri's experience were happening to me. I stood before myself and endured every moment of the pain I'd caused her—I felt in equal measure my emotions as the little girl behaving cruelly to her friend and Sherri's feelings as she grew into more hurt. All the while I witnessed this scene from a place of higher consciousness—where my real regret lived.

This was the first of a lifetime of moments. I was held accountable for all of my actions, thoughts, and words, one-by-one.

I re-lived and faced each important moment up until the age of 29. Vacillating between the anguish of my mistakes and an overwhelming sense of deep love depending on whether my actions were kind or cruel.

Each moment played out from both my perspective and the other person's—while my consciousness remained enfolded in a blanket of unconditional love—totally free of judgment.

Despite that tremendous all-encompassing love and support, when I saw that I had made a mistake, the pain from it felt inescapable and so absolutely unbearable that I never wanted to make a mistake like that again—even hurting Sherri's feelings during our early childhood years.

I understood and felt which moments brought me closer to living in the truth of who I am as a Divine Soul and which moments pulled me away from it. This was the purpose of my life review.

When my review ended, there was only love.

A powerful vibration of unconditional love filled every ounce of my being until I couldn't tell myself apart from it. I realized and experienced myself as divine love and the illusion of separateness became an impossible dream.

How did I ever believe myself to be separate from this love? This love was more real and permanent than any human experience.

From this experience I had, I believe the life review is meant to teach us about our strengths and weaknesses. There isn't a single moment of life that goes unnoticed or that doesn't matter. Everything counts and we're accountable for every single moment of our lives—so death is not something to be afraid of but rather to be prepared for.

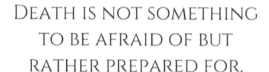

DEATH IS NOT SOMETHING
TO BE AFRAID OF BUT
RATHER PREPARED FOR.

Chapter 3

Gifts Beyond the Veil

As my journey continued, I became aware of being in the presence of four highly advanced souls. The most powerful divine bliss, peace, and unconditional love permeated my Soul until I was conscious of nothing else. I couldn't so much see these four great souls with my eyes, or what I had known as eyes, as I could see them with my Soul. They had no physical appearance I could describe, just a vast presence of God consciousness, wisdom, and an overwhelming divine love.

Upon meeting them, I merged with an infinitely expanding bliss, love, joy and peace—the most natural feeling I have ever experienced. I realized myself as the Soul, shedding all illusion of the roles I had played on Earth.

Everything I believed and thought of as Mariko fell away effortlessly—from seeing myself as female to thinking I had a name. My relationships, favorite foods, career, and even love of rock climbing all faded. All concepts of who I had been and my personal insecurities disappeared. I was free to be me—without any earthly perceptions of who I was or should be.

I soared in the infinite bliss of God's love, free of the limiting constraints of time. Hours, weeks, and years all stretched out into infinity—the only true time.

Then, the souls spoke, but not with human words in the way we are accustomed to. They communicated through a means infinitely clearer than words. It felt like being uploaded with information I would need. Rather than an upload from computer-to-computer via the internet, this came soul-to-soul by way of infinite consciousness and love.

At this point I became focused, acutely aware of—and concentrated deeply on—the silent connection with these great souls. I wasn't cognizant of the details they gave me at the time, just as you wouldn't be aware of the contents of a box someone hands you until you later looked inside. I knew this wasn't something I had to understand right then, but instead I would access it later.

When my upload finished, I experienced an air of deep peace all around. A stillness filled my being along with the responsibility to share what I had just been given.

I stayed connected to these divine souls in what felt like an ocean of infinite consciousness. I had no awareness of time or space—only of the truth—that I was, I am, one with infinite consciousness. And—that everyone else is one with this infinite consciousness, too.

Subtly, I became aware of myself again—separate from infinity but still filled with peace, bliss, and joy.

I basked in this experience when, suddenly, an intense, small, white light blazed in the distance and captured my attention. It pulled me further away from infinity. As the light grew in diameter, I saw a silhouette in the shape of a person slowly floating downward, getting closer and closer to what appeared to be some kind of entrance. "Who is that?" I asked.

"It's the part of you that gets attached," the beings replied.

The silhouette coasted deliberately—slowly—until it reached the brilliant light. We watched in silence until it disappeared through a tunnel-like opening.

Before the beings spoke again, this time with human words, I sensed a powerful current of what I have come to call "thought waves."

Because words alone seemed inadequate to convey their message of joy, I sensed the vibration of their meaning and it carried through to me in what felt like waves of thought.

If I had still been in my physical body, I think I would have exploded with their infinite joy. I remained conscious now only of joy. While the peace, love, and bliss were still so present, I became part of the infinitely expanding divine joy which permeates the universe.

Everyone I had ever loved felt a part of me—as if we were one. I knew no sense of time in the linear way we experience it on Earth. It felt as if I were in this state of ever-expanding joy for months, for years, for eons. "I am free," I thought. "I am alive. I am joy. I was never Mariko! I always have been and always will be divine joy. I could never be anything else." As this realization filled my consciousness, I abandoned all ego identification and merged with my truest Self as infinite love, joy, peace, and bliss. "I am bliss!"

Then I heard—or felt, "It's not your time. You have to go back." Their words and thought waves coaxed me with love.

"No."

They spoke again gently, lovingly, "You have to go back and help people. Remember who you are. Go back and help them."

I replied with the vibration of resistance—a thought wave of "No, I want to stay here, I'm home now."

They nudged me again. Their sweet divine voices filled my consciousness, "Each soul has its appointed time to transition out of life on earth. You can't go before or after your time; it's not possible. It's not your time. You have to go back. Go back and help people. Remember who you are."

Waves of love filled my being and I immediately obeyed, making an effort of sheer will to get back into my physical body, wanting nothing more than to serve.

Nothing happened.

"I can't get back in my body," I said. Still floating in the divine joy, peace, love, and bliss I felt a push from behind. An enormous force hurled me through infinite space.

I took a breath.

It hurt.

I hurt.

I felt an excruciating pain from head to toe, as if I'd been crushed to pieces by that iron weight, lit on fire, and mercilessly kept alive.

I screamed wordlessly, "I need to go to the hospital."

As soon as I'd thought it, the pain was gone and I returned to those divine souls, floating in expansive peace.

"Don't use western medicine," they said with both words and thought waves. I remained immersed in divine love until their message sank in and it all made sense to me—not on a level I could describe with words. I just understood that what I was to go through couldn't be resolved by allopathic medicine.

Another breath...then pain. I felt completely drained. I sensed something touching my face. As I floated back into consciousness, I realized it was Chris, and he was slapping my face. "Mariko! Wake up! Mariko!"

I worked on coming back into my body enough to open my eyes a tiny bit. I couldn't move. I couldn't speak. I just breathed, cracked open my eyes, and looked at my husband's face. Time came to a stop and the peace of the afterworld remained with me.

"Where'd you go?"

"I died," I whispered.

I lay there with my husband beside me and conveyed in a whisper the message I just received about not using Western medicine. There is no doubt in my eternal Soul that what these divine souls told me was to keep me on my life's path. I wouldn't die if I stayed home and didn't go to a hospital. They wouldn't let me. It wasn't my time.

An aura of divine peace and sacredness permeated our small home as I put into words the journey I had just traveled. My heart overflowed with pure love. Even though Chris had just found me lying in bed, still, not breathing, my skin a shade of grey, he didn't panic.

That divine grace had extended to him as well.

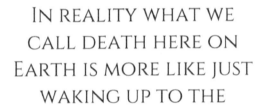

IN REALITY WHAT WE
CALL DEATH HERE ON
EARTH IS MORE LIKE JUST
WAKING UP TO THE
TRUTH OF WHO YOU ARE.

Chapter 4

Soul Priority

My instructions were clear: Remember who you are. Go back and help people.

I remember. I've always remembered. Just at you might easily remember your wedding day or your high school graduation, I remembered my last lifetime and my life in-between physical incarnations. I had always believed that everyone could do this. My memories are a part of who I am.

It wasn't until I was 18 that I realized not everyone remembered the time before they incarnated; most people don't. I used to talk about it when I was a child. When people ignored me or looked at me funny, I assumed it was just taboo to speak of. How could I know any different? I was born like that.

My most vivid memory began centuries ago when I was a man in Europe. I felt then as anyone would feel as if standing near a window in a modern high-rise apartment today. My house was a two-story stone building. There were no ornate markings, just the stone building, and there was another one across a narrow dirt road outdoors at ground level. I stood before that window watching a merchant pull a handcart down the narrow road. The room was cool but not cold enough for a fire— yet I felt frozen—numb. I focused on the merchant while a mix of jealousy and shock prodded at my heart. He was living an ordinary life and would continue pulling that cart every day before returning home to his wife and three daughters. I, on the other hand, had been instrumental in building and keeping up the town's windmill. I always made sure my community got what they needed, from food to farm equipment. I felt important and needed. Yet I was dying, and the merchant was going to live.

There was no cure for the disease I suffered, and I didn't have much time left. Although I'd been ill for several months, I refused to seek help or advice. I had too much to do, and a child to live for. Her mother had died. The child and I were each other's entire world—and that world couldn't continue if we were torn apart.

I realized my daughter wouldn't be totally alone. My sister would care for her. Their bond was already forming—tentatively—as neither aimed to hurt me with their connection. I made an effort to appear contented about their future together—it was all for show. My heart was being ripped from my chest and I could take only the most minimal comfort for their situation. My daughter would be safe and cared for, but it wouldn't be the same.

My daughter remained locked by my side for weeks, heartbroken and helpless to stop me from leaving her. She held my hand so tightly it felt as if she intended to tether me to this life—our life.

I spent our last days together telling her again and again how much I loved her, hoping she could carry my love with her. As we talked, I memorized the details of her face. She had straight blond hair that flowed almost to her waist, fair skin, and pink cheeks—usually not streaked with tears as they were then. She was slender and tall for her age and seemed to always glow with a soft pastel pink energy. I attributed that to her youth but thought perhaps she would always have a pink glow.

My daughter's big blue-grey eyes watched over me day and night. She catered to my every need—working hard as both daughter and nurse. My heart beamed with pride. I took in her transition—right before my eyes—from the little girl I remembered into the woman she was becoming. While most children were mature back then, losing her mother made her grow up even faster. Gratitude welled up inside my heart for the glimpse of this new side of her.

As the time for my final transition out of this world drew closer, I spent all of my time in bed. Friends visited and left but my daughter remained my constant companion, my love. Eventually, I became unable to respond but I still knew what went on around me. My cherished daughter by my side, my sister and other friends several feet away, standing near the wall of my room talking quietly.

Then it began—the process of death. I was calm, unafraid, and the process felt familiar. The room became extremely bright although my eyes were closed—my breath grew shallow. I felt no pain, just silence and peace until my life review began.

Floating in the dark infinite space I saw it all, my accomplishments, and regrets. The regrets felt so painful. I didn't regret anything earthly. I had many outstanding achievements. Yet I experienced tremendous pain upon seeing the choices before me and witnessing what I preferred. Each time I had a spiritual opportunity before me, I chose the earthly path instead.

I had the opportunity to go deeper into spirituality and raise my consciousness, but I chose earthly accomplishments. Each time I had a chance to listen to my intuition, I chose reason. I always chose what was easier for me. I never hurt anyone, but I never tried to advance my consciousness, either.

It was in the little details of my life where I got my priorities wrong; thousands of moments all pointing in one direction. When I gave someone advice, I would push away my intuitive feeling and go with what was practical. Often my practical advice worked out fine, but later I realized that my intuition would have provided a better outcome. It became so obvious in my daily life that I was meant to listen to my intuition that many times I resolved to try—only to fall back on old habits. It was a pattern I was comfortable in and felt my consistent success was more important than trying out an unknown factor using my intuition. Reason never let me down.

Only during my life review did I see the other side of my choices. How things could have gone if I had been receptive to my spiritual path, beginning with my intuition.

I wasn't being asked to abandon reason, just to listen to my intuition as well. The very best moments were when reason and intuition were in alignment. However, I just focused on the facts, never giving my spiritual side any credit. In every case, it would have worked out better for those I was helping and myself if I had surrendered to and credited my intuition.

I couldn't help but feel that I had wasted so many divine opportunities. I could have done more. I could have made better decisions. I could have grown spiritually. "I'll do it. Send me back, I understand now!"

"You can't go back. You died. You can never be that person again, it's too late."
The finality of their words slammed into me and I floated in the vibration of my own regret. I vowed to never make that mistake again.

Finished with my life review, I was unwilling to move on. I paused between my life review and my journey to the next world. From there, I could see her again, my daughter. She was alone, curled up and crying in her bed, as I watched over her from what felt like above, looking down. Her pain was my pain and we grieved together. I missed her terribly. I missed my life, but the only trace of that old life that held any meaning was my relationship to my daughter. I stayed as long as possible watching over her manage life without my physical presence.

At first, it felt as if she sensed me with her—like an unspoken secret between us. She would pause in the middle of doing something, like washing clothes, eating, or as she fell asleep. She'd get quiet and—for a moment—we would share in our love. Did she know I watched over her? I had no voice but wanted nothing more than to scream out, "I'm here. I love you."

I lived in a state free of time. My sole engagement was to watch over my daughter and the remnants of my last life. Only, I wasn't part of that life anymore. Little by little her pain eased, and her thoughts weren't as focused on me.

I found myself tuning into the peace that surrounded me more often than watching my daughter—until the pull of what would be my next step felt more real than remaining in that state of stationary existence. My daughter was living her life, and it became time to go live mine.

Chapter 5

Life in the Afterlife

The afterlife takes place in what's known as the astral world. It's a world made exclusively of light and it is where most of us go after we die. I wrote "most" because only the true enlightened souls get to go to the higher realms of heaven. Only those who have worked to attain soul consciousness, or even God consciousness, get to bypass the astral world. A soul goes to the place that befits their consciousness—which is the astral for most people—but there are much higher realms. There are lower realms, too.

I found myself standing in a new world made of light and immediately became aware an overwhelming wave of timeless bliss, joy, and love that washed through my new body. I was home.

I opened my eyes but couldn't see clearly—my surroundings appeared blurry, and the colors were muted as if a soft white blanket of light covered everything. I felt a pressure on my forehead and knew immediately what to do—I opened my spiritual eye. I can't say exactly how I did it, I just focused on it and suddenly I could see out of it. It felt like a perfectly natural thing to do.

I stood absolutely still absorbed the spectacular beauty of a new variety of astral colors unknown to me before that moment. As I looked at my surroundings, I found that I was standing in a large field—everything was made of light—the grass under my feet, forest trees all around, a river off to my left and the mountains beyond it. It was an entire luminescent world, filled with vibrant wonderful new colors, and the air was infused with unconditional love.

After a short while, I attempted to move. My new body felt incredible! I was made entirely of light along with the rest of this world.

I felt no pain, no tension, no fatigue, just pure expansive joy.

My astral body appeared to be neither male nor female. I was simply a soul encased in a magnificent body of light. Concepts of male and female didn't exist here the same way they do on Earth. If someone had been female in a past life and identified with looking female, that soul's astral body could appear female. But it could just as easily appear male if that soul wanted it to. I have no idea what I appeared like to other the souls in this world, but whatever sex I appeared I never felt female or male. I was simply me.

While absorbed in the love, joy, and bliss of this new world, I became aware of a new sensation arising from my body as I was standing in the brilliant colors of the astral field. A group of people approached me, and as they neared, I became aware of a pressure building inside of my throat.

My heart filled with joy—I recognized these souls and the roles they had played in my last life.

One of them was a soul I had known for many lifetimes; someone who had recently been my wife. This welcome and joyous reunion exploded the bliss within me, and I felt ecstatic. My throat chakra continued to build in pressure until I relaxed the area and my thoughts soundlessly poured out. We could easily communicate this way, a clear perception of our thoughts and emotions emanated out of our throat and heart chakras and we understood each other with more clarity than words—conveying the love and gratitude we had for each other. We didn't do any small talk or catch up on our lives, we just embraced. That was enough.

I became aware of being encircled by my loved ones, each waiting to greet me. The first group was from my most recent lifetime—

my parents, grandparents, uncles, aunts, and a few friends. Then more souls came; ones that I had been close to in previous lifetimes—family and friends and sometimes even animals.

It was a time of joyous reunion with my loved ones. Everyone I ever knew was there, and we were engulfed in the purest divine love. I didn't have to look for them, they were all nearby with open arms and open hearts filled with joy.

With those I loved, our love was intense, pure, and our reunion that much sweeter. As we embraced, our hearts and consciousnesses filled completely with pure love and joy. Time seemed to stand still. For those with whom I'd had issues with in my previous life, there was an understanding and gratitude because it was through that relationship that I learned some of my most treasured lessons.

Each moment of sweet reunion was filled with the most explosive feeling of joy. I was even reunited with old friends who hadn't shared the most recent incarnation with me.

In some cases, I met souls that had incarnated during the same lifetime I'd just had, but we didn't know each other while on Earth. One of those friends greeted me and I distinctly remember teasing him (he'd been a man in his last life).

"You were famous last time!" I said.

"Yes" he replied, with an air of embarrassment.

Being famous doesn't mean anything once you're back in the astral world; only spiritual progress does. So, my old friend was just fulfilling his desire to play the role of a famous person and was slightly embarrassed when I brought it up because the reality that only spiritual progress matters was universally understood there. We had a laugh about it anyway.

One of my favorite reunions was not with a person at all, but with an animal. We recognized each other immediately and embraced. My dear friend wasn't in the horse and cat forms I had known in previous incarnations on Earth but in a human form on this side.

This was one of the purest and most uncomplicated loves of all and there was a tremendous feeling of love and gratitude as we embraced once again. These greetings went on and on and I was filled with pure joy and bliss! I was home, I was alive!

In reality what we call death here on Earth is more like just waking up to the truth of who you are.

Everything was different now that I'd had a life-into-death experience. How I related to this world was different. Instead of using my physical body and its five senses, I was learning to rely on the anatomy of my astral body. The first and most important part of my experience was learning about my chakras—seven energy centers that allowed me to function in my new body of light. I had already used one upon arriving there—my sixth charka, or spiritual eye.

I needed that to see. The pressure at my throat was from my fifth chakra—the throat chakra and the love pouring out of my chest upon seeing my loved ones emanated from my fourth chakra—the heart chakra.

Of the seven chakras, I tuned into those three higher centers for most of my stay in the astral realm. These energy centers serve much the same way our organs function in our physical bodies. They are part of our anatomy in the astral world and I wouldn't have gotten as far as I did without them.

When all those sweet reunions came to a close, I did what came natural for me—I took a nap. It's what many souls do between lifetimes. We live our lives here on Earth, learn to align with our souls, according to our karma and desires, then go back to the astral world and spend some time in a peaceful sleep. Less evolved souls may sleep for most or all of their time in the astral world before reincarnating into the physical world, while other more evolved souls can skip the period of sleep all together.

It was my choice to nap. I found a nice space in what I can only describe as the astral woods. It was a tiny oval meadow of luminescent grass and flowers. This meadow was surrounded by brilliant, tall astral trees near a beautiful, glowing stream, and there was a tall mountain range in the distance. The flowers in this little meadow glowed day and night with the familiar colors of yellows, pinks, and blues, along with astral colors that are unseen on Earth. As I lay on the bright green grass of the meadow, I felt safer and more at home than I could recall. A peaceful bliss came over me and I fell into a deep slumber.

I awoke to find my spiritual teacher standing over me. I intuitively knew who he was and that he was checking to see if I was ready yet— but I was having an incredibly epic nap. I peeked up at him, feeling the bliss of this new world, but then a blanket of peace coaxed me into remaining asleep.

I have no idea if he came by every five minutes or every five months since there was no linear time to measure anything by. He tried several times to wake me up—and without fail I peeked up at him through my spiritual eye and chose sleep. I felt sedated by the bliss—even if I had wanted to wake up, I don't think I could have. Once I had snoozed long enough, I found my teacher standing on the edge of the meadow and I walked toward him. We communicated using the regular means in this world—our chakras.

Now when I think of it, the closest explanation humans have on Earth to describe our conversation would be the concept of mental telepathy—but it was much clearer than that. It was a way of packing in every detail of thought, emotion, big picture, short-term goals, long-term goals, and the truth of my being through a vibration that took only a few moments.

What became clear to me after our meeting was that it was time for me to get to work.

Not work in the sense of employment (although eventually I did help other souls as a healer there) but work on raising my consciousness, work on attaining my own enlightenment, and work on uniting my consciousness with God's consciousness.

At first, I was tormented by my past decisions of earthy goals over spiritual ones and my astral heart filled with a burning regret each time I thought of it. I had allowed such magnificent opportunities to slip by.

Now, each day my entire focus was on my spiritual life and communing with God.

Occasionally someone would visit me who needed healing and they would lay down in that little meadow of light while I sat beside them and cleared the energy or emotion they wanted to release. Then, I went back to my efforts to commune with God. I didn't socialize much. I watched a group of souls with higher consciousness who were nearby and wanted so very much to spend my days with them, but I wasn't able to. It was as if it was understood—the less conscious souls (or, the more ego-attached souls) could not hang out with the higher consciousness souls until they were ready. It just didn't happen, and after the monumental error of not using my intuition more in my last life, I didn't really want to spend time with souls who were my equals, so I chose solitude most of the time.

Occasionally I would feel hungry. That sensation wasn't the same as on Earth because I didn't have a physical stomach or a metabolism. I would feel my energy body get tired, so I'd eat the light-filled astral fruits that grew on the trees. The sweet astral nectar was all I needed to sustain and charge my body of light, which was unreservedly satisfying, but never something I felt the need to over-indulge in. Imagine living off of a complete food that never leaves you wanting for more, is perfectly balanced to your body's needs, and tastes like your all-time favorite food. It was that good.

Each time I ate I'd experience a deep appreciation for how amazing it was that I never needed or wanted more than it took to recharge my energy. Once I thought of food, it just appeared; I didn't have to find it. I would just manifest it in my hand, ready to eat. Sometimes I would choose to pick fruit off of a tree but usually I just manifested it.

This also meant I rarely left the meadow. I spent my astral days and nights communing with God in deep meditation, and through my efforts I was shedding the identity of my last life and making some spiritual progress. This is what led to me being able to socialize with the group of higher conscious souls I had wanted to be with upon my arrival. Now I could leave my beautiful astral meadow and commune with those who became my dearest friends. I wasn't ready before, but I enjoyed it now. I had a small spiritual community to relate to and I was quite content for a while.

On occasion I would feel the pull to leave the astral world and travel to an even higher realm.

All it would take to travel was willing into existence a light at my feet-like a circular platform that was part of a long beam of light reaching to the place I desired to travel to. Once I stepped on it, I'd travel through the astral air and into the world I wanted to go. I'd have to return within a time period that I could feel. No one told me my stay was limited, I just knew. My vibration wasn't yet high enough to stay in the higher realm I was visiting.

I was enjoying my life in this realm and had a sense of fulfillment. I had a community of friends, my astral meadow, and plenty of food. It was so wonderful. And yet, one day as I was walking to meet my friends at our usual place by the river, I felt a subtle nagging in my heart. I wasn't sure what it was at first, but it wouldn't go away. Each day I would have my routine of meditation and communion with my friends, but the nagging feeling became heavier and heavier. I knew I needed to face it, but I admit I delayed until I couldn't stand it anymore.

Of course, I knew what it was. I had a strong intuition and could only ignore it for so long. I didn't want to look at it because I was happy and I didn't want anything to change. But there it was, the truth was staring me down, my priorities were all wrong, and I was repeating my same old mistakes again. I had built a life in the astral world. I was finding fulfillment outside of my true self and had built a daily routine around it.

I realized that just because I thought of some souls as being of a higher consciousness when I first arrived, it didn't mean they were enlightened. In fact, I realized that it was best to stay in solitude so as to not get caught up in playing the role of an advanced spiritual person in the astral world.

With my priorities straight, and a rather large dose of humility, I returned to my light filled meadow to renew my efforts for spiritual progress. This time I wasn't going to get distracted from my soul's true purpose—to merge with God. Day and night, year after year, I sat or stood in that meadow, communing with God until my consciousness could swim in the infinite ocean of God's love. I was in bliss consciousness, but I hadn't merged with God.

Enlightenment, or liberation, is beyond feeling the bliss and so long as I was experiencing both myself and bliss, I was to some degree separate from it. I couldn't get beyond it—but I wanted to more than anything and was willing to do whatever it took to go there.

As my time in the astral world drew to a close, I recall a special meeting with my spiritual teacher. It felt as if—just by his presence—every particle of light in my body was vibrating at a super speed and transforming me with God's radiant love. That day there were four of us standing together, planning our next steps and earthly incarnation. In front of me was my teacher and to my right was the soul who would be my husband. Standing slightly behind me and to my left was the soul who would be our child.

The air was charged with an excitement and celebration for my next step and departure from the astral realm. This moment with my spiritual teacher was the high point of my sojourn to the astral world after my life as that man in Europe.

Chapter 6

The Causal World

No longer in my astral body with a familiar human shape, I had become light—a purple light to be specific—but I was still me. This light body is the most subtle of all our forms. When I shed my astral body, I went into the higher realm of the causal world. This is the thought world, not a world as we know it—as in a round planet made of physical matter, or even the astral world made of light. The causal world is one of thought and idea. There is no physical shape to the causal world that I could discern, no sound or heightened vibrations of divine joy, and no linear time. I was aware of other souls around me but there was no contact with them, no warm embraces or sweet reunions, no blissful experiences. We were there to work. The social niceties of the astral world were not necessary here. I knew another opportunity was upon me.

At first all I did was look at the surroundings—and not with my astral spiritual eye that I'd grown so accustomed to, but with my consciousness. I spent some time reaching out to the other souls but to no avail, they were not there to socialize. My neighbors seemed to be in various states of conscious growth, although there were no low-vibration souls there. Every being was working and totally focused—on what I didn't know yet. Some were very high souls who were vibrating only bliss and they appeared in my consciousness as colorful lights. A few souls appeared grey, and to me it seemed that they were feeling...angry...maybe tormented.

Further away, there were more souls who were quite advanced, very ancient, and operating on a level beyond my full understanding. They felt like a forest of ancient souls. I was not there to do the exact same thing as they were doing. I was there to purify myself.

Then it began. I suppose that being in a world of thought, it made sense that there was only one thing to do: Think. This was a world of consciousness, and I was there to continue to purify my own consciousness. Aside from the most ancient souls, that's what everyone around me was doing there.

Those whom I sensed were higher conscious souls were just further along in their own purification process, and those in whom I sensed anger were just working out their karma in order to purify themselves. The soul is encased by the physical, astral, and causal bodies which house our karma and desires. Each of us must purify our desires and karma to reach final liberation, or enlightenment, and that is all I wanted.

It didn't start out well for me. Soon I understood why some souls felt tormented. I was consumed with regret from the mistakes of my most recent incarnation. I chose my own earthy desires when I had been given opportunities for real spiritual growth. I knew the possibilities were there and I didn't choose them; sometimes I even ignored the pull from my intuition for the comfort of my own physical desires. I felt the burden of my mistakes on a level so deep that the regret of my life review after I died seemed almost easy. That burning regret I felt in my heart in the astral world now felt like child's play, and I was stuck in it. I had no physical body in which to work out my karma. I couldn't sprain an ankle, get sick, or go through the drama of a strained relationship in order to work out my karma physically. Earth held endless opportunities to work out my karma on a level unavailable to me now, and I am conscious of all my errors from that life. Each and every opportunity was played out and I again experienced the mistakes I'd made in that lifetime.

This was the purification process—understanding my mistakes and being fully immersed in the vibration of my own deep regret and pain until that regret and pain had become purified in the light of my own soul's consciousness. When that process was complete, there was only peace. I had purified myself of my mistakes and would not repeat that particular error again. I vowed that the next time the Divine Mother gives me an opportunity, I'm taking it. No questions, no hesitations.

I stayed in that quiet peace until the image in my consciousness changed and I realized I was being shown the nature of human incarnations. I saw souls leaving the physical realm and going to the place best befitting their consciousness. The majority of souls on earth go to the astral world. Some souls who were very evil during their incarnation went to one of the lower realms.

Highly advanced souls went straight to the causal world, but my focus was on the time someone made it directly to God.

I could see souls going from the physical realm to God. Directly! Not many souls, but I saw it was possible. They completely bypassed the astral and causal realms and merged directly with God. Once I saw this was a possibility, I wanted it. I've never wanted anything so badly as I wanted this. For the first time in my whole life—in any life—I was witnessing something worth wanting, and the only desire worth having. "They have done it!" I thought, "they reached enlightenment on the physical realm. I WANT THAT. Whatever it takes, whatever I have to go through, I want that!"

"I WANT THE HIGHER TEACHINGS." I call again and again, pleading with our Divine Creator, "I want the higher teachings." I appeal with my entire soul, "I want the higher teachings." It's all I'm conscious of now, all I'm focused on, "I WANT THE HIGHER TEACHINGS."

There was no linear time, but my pleas felt endless; my entire being was focused on just one fact: I wanted the higher teachings that could bring me directly to God. That thought expanded in all directions and I pleaded over and over again.

"I WANT THE HIGHER TEACHINGS. I WANT THE HIGHER TEACHINGS! I WANT THE HIGHER TEACHINGS!!"

It became quiet again, and I was back in a life review, but not like the one I'd had before the astral realm. This is different. This is the beginning, my beginning. I am starting off in my earliest incarnation. Divine Mother must have heard my incessant demands for the higher teachings, and like a loving parent, She is giving me the opportunity to earn it. So, I begin an enormous life review as a purification process that begins with my first incarnation on Earth and ends with my most recent one.

My entire existence as a soul is to be reviewed.

In this state, I learned that I've had millions of lifetimes, but I started out in the lowest form as an insect. I had no real consciousness except instinct. It was like being in a machine, and my only concern was how to operate that machine. Where were the controls, I wondered, and how do I operate it?

There were many different machines in many different lifetimes, sometimes crawling sometimes flying. Once I entered the animal kingdom, I spent many lifetimes both on the ground and flying.

In one lifetime, I awoke to a feeling of warm air and an earthy scent. I was safe, warm, and knew my mother was in the nest with me. Simply knowing she was there satisfied my instinct for survival, and I was content. That is, until it was time to leave the nest. I remember feeling apprehensive. I was the second to last to leave the nest, but instinct took over and before I knew it, my little body was soaring through the air. I was a little wobbly at first, but I did it! I felt so free and spent several lifetimes enjoying the wind under my wings, hunting for food, finding a mate, and raising babies. Animal life after animal life, I was always driven by instinct but became a little more aware of the me behind the instinct each time.

Then the feeling shifted. I was having a conscious life—meaning I saw myself as an individual who had responsibilities outside of my own needs and instincts. The ground was covered in snow, and I was safe with my family.

I loved wintertime and felt so alive as the snow crunched beneath my paws. I was a wolf. My pack and I operated as one system, each needing the other to survive, but the unbreakable bond between us went far beyond mere survival. I was responsible for keeping everyone in line and if they broke the rules, they would have to answer to me. Although I was big, very tough, and commanded respect from my pack, I wasn't the alpha. That role wasn't made for me and I was quite content with my place in the pack. We loved each other and shared an absolute commitment, duty, loyalty, and trust. The other wolves were my family, my home, and the bond we shared allowed us to function as if we were one being.

Then the review of my human lifetimes began and along with it the revelations of my deeper lessons. I was so lost. I didn't start out as a highly conscious person seeking the spiritual truths of the Universe. I remember feeling bewildered at how some people seemed to have such an easy time in life, as if they understood something that I had yet to learn and I often felt like an outsider. I spent a lot of time quietly watching people interacting with each other and learning from them.

They were so much more comfortable and at ease with themselves, each other, and this world than I was. They were even able to take on more complex jobs than I was and, at first, I saw them as more intelligent than I was. Eventually—after several lifetimes—I began to seek out what I thought was the goal of life based on what my exposure had been to that point: to fulfill my desires and have a good time enjoying my physical senses. It seems shallow, I know, but there it was, and along with it came pain. In one lifetime, I was only concerned with money and became very rich, while in another incarnation I mostly gratified my senses in any way I could, my favorite indulgence then was food. Incarnation after incarnation I slowly and reluctantly learned from my mistakes. The most lonesome lifetime I had was as a soldier in a castle somewhere cold, damp, and grey. I lived amongst other men but felt utterly alone. My life felt pointless and totally empty. No family, no friends, no love, just endless days and nights enduring the cold, damp, wet and grey skies. I was always cold, and my body constantly ached.

As each lifetime passed and I learned a little more, my incarnations became purposeful. I began focusing my life around both my family and material success, attempting all the while to be a good person. Occasionally I would really make a big mistake and spend a future incarnation purifying myself through a series of hardships and lessons. Over thousands of lifetimes, I evolved enough through the process of trial and error, pain and love, until I finally began to further my spiritual growth by seeking the Divine Truth.

Reviewing my lifetimes from a higher perspective allowed me to experience bliss after a lifetime of trying to reach God, and the anguish of a lifetime seeking only material gratification. Eventually the feelings of bliss and anguish came in equal measure, and I recognized the ways in which I conducted myself. In some lives I was honest, moral, and kind; in others I allowed greed and frustration to lead me. Yet it was always the lifetimes where I chose alignment with my soul qualities that I was happiest. My lifetimes were a mix of both and not all were on the planet we call earth, but most were.

After witnessing each lifetime, I again reviewed the choices I'd made, feeling the bliss of my soul aligned choices and the pain of my selfish ego driven choices. On and on this went, reviewing each and every lifetime from my very beginning until it was time to purify them all.   As souls, we are above all karma, both good and bad but we can purify ourselves of both in order to reach final liberation, and my incessant demands to Divine Mother for the higher teachings brought on my own opportunity for purification. I knew I was being given a chance for spiritual growth and that it would be difficult, but I remembered my vow to say yes to any and all of God's opportunities.

Apparently, the best way for me to burn up that karma was to go through what felt like a lifetime of infinite pain—in the causal world, without a physical or astral body. The pain of my past decisions and actions began to build up to a point where I could do nothing to alleviate it. I was in a body of pure thought and consciousness and the only way to work through the pain was to merge with it.

My entire consciousness was focused on the all-encompassing pain, and I screamed. Not for help.

Not for it to stop. I just screamed. It was the only vehicle for me to work out this level of pain. I didn't have a voice to make any sounds with, so I screamed mentally. It was my only thought; my entire consciousness was enveloped in this one scream. It was all I could do, and it went on for so long that it became...me. That pain, my scream, and I—we were all one and then I couldn't even remember why I was in that pain. I just merged with it, as if I had been thrown into a huge forest fire and instead of dying to escape the pain of the fire, I became the flame all the while feeling and merging with the pain of my past actions. Occasionally I would separate my consciousness from the infinite pain just to see if it looked like it might end soon—but no—it wasn't ending. It felt like a hundred years that I went through that process of purification.

At long last, the pain began to ease and I was beginning to feel a hint of peace in my consciousness. "Is it over, am I done?" The scream continued to die down until there were no thoughts, no screaming, no pain, just peace. Absolute peace.

My consciousness filled with the most beautiful golden light expanding into infinity.

Divine peace became bliss, no thoughts, just eternal bliss. I was home. I remained united in this most extraordinary expansive bliss consciousness, free of time and space, until my next lesson.

The scene in my consciousness changed once again, and I was being given a glimpse of the cosmic reality.

There is a God. Not in the way some religions have taught, but God is real, not a man sitting on a cloud in heaven waiting to judge us. God is more than any limited idea we can conceive of. God is infinite consciousness. Infinite, as in never began and will never end, ever. It's easy to say but hard to comprehend, even for me and I saw it—no, I experienced it. But still, infinite, always, and never can be` hard to wrap our human minds around. Our experiences in the physical world are so finite that it seems nothing lasts forever. And here on Earth, it doesn't. But our lives aren't limited to the physical realm. We continue on, incarnation-after-incarnation, until we are liberated from the physical world. Then, we keep going on to the higher realms and sometimes chose to come back and help people in the physical world.

We have no birth or death because as divine souls, we are part of God (children of God, pieces of God) and as such, we are infinite, too. Just as a drop of water in the ocean isn't separate from the ocean, human souls are always connected to God's infinite consciousness.

To what degree you are aware of your oneness with God is what determines your incarnations. The physical, astral, and causal realms aren't the only realms; there are much higher vibration worlds and much lower ones. During my between-lives experiences, the highest realm was not even conceivable to me. I knew it was there, but I couldn't have a thought about it. That realm was far too high above my consciousness, and I understood that there were very few souls who could conceive of it.

My most profound realization was that our human conception of God is just that—human. God is more than we can conceive of with our human consciousness, but God is knowable. It takes soul consciousness to connect with God and even then, there's more. God is infinite consciousness so it's impossible to conceive of something infinite with our finite human consciousness—but you aren't limited to your humanness. Attaining enlightenment from the physical, astral, and causal realms are very possible, but that's not the end. There is no cosmic retirement, no place where your soul is not needed anymore. You will always be necessary to the divine plan—and there is a plan.

I soared in the infinite knowledge of cosmic consciousness while merged in an endless golden light of bliss. From here I was able to experience the universe and feel all beings in it. I watched entire planets of souls and would occasionally focus in on one soul. I witnessed the entire process of birth till death of many souls on many worlds until my own divine plan unfolded once more.

I had been united in perfect bliss for so long that I had forgotten anything else. But now, I felt different. Oh, I still felt bliss and love but, I was different. There was so much love. It felt as if my heart could explode with love. That was it! That was the difference, I had a heart...I had a body again.

I AM—LIKE YOU—HERE TO
FULFILL MY SOUL
ASSIGNMENT. A TASK THAT
WILL FRIGHTEN YOU LIKE
NO OTHER AND FREE YOU
TO BECOME THE PERSON
YOU'RE MEANT TO BE.

PART II:

The Four Soul Archetypes

Chapter 7

Who Am I in this Lifetime?

If there's one thing that's true about me, it's that I don't listen. My dad said it a million times when I was growing up: "You just don't listen. Why don't you listen?" He was usually just trying to keep me from hurting myself, like the time he told me not to touch a hot motor and I immediately touched it as soon as he turned his back. Of course, I burned my finger.

As a child, I had no words to tell him I was not listening to him, or anyone else in the world around me, because I could hear. There was more to listen to and learn from that came from within than I could ever learn from what seemed to be the 'real' world.

Today, it's in the gift of not listening to what the world says I should do to be successful and happy that allows me to live and work in total alignment with what I'm here to do as a spiritual healer, teacher, and mentor.

I've developed my own signature work where I help my clients by bringing them into the higher astral and causal realms through my technique called Highertherapy™. My clients are able to receive the answers they need to live their soul assignment, heal deep SOUL ARCHETPYE wounds, decondition their limited human beliefs and even align their work or business with their soul.

My path to living the assignment I'd chosen for my life wasn't always clear. It began—as it does for most of us—with one harmless question: "What do you want to be when you grow up?"

Only four years old when I was asked this very adult question for the first time, I knew I wanted to get the answer right. I smiled and didn't say a word.

In that moment, I was showing them who I was by radiating my best smile and feelings of love and joy.

They asked again. "What do you want to be when you grow up?"

Now I was confused. Didn't they feel all the love I was giving off? The love of my soul and the best of what I'll be when I grow up?

I smiled again but this time let out a giggle. The love and joy of my soul were expanding around me. They had to have felt it!

No. They just stared at me, waiting for an answer.

To this day I don't know where I got the word, but I looked directly at them and blurted out an answer: "Physicist!"

Everyone erupted in cheers of approval and gave me hugs. Two things became clear to me. First, I'd gotten the answer right, and would now have to be a physicist.

Second, I'd have to become something other than me to get such effusive love and approval.

Being me wasn't enough.

I learned something very important about being a grown up in that moment: that I was supposed to disconnect what I do from who I am.

Many of us have learned this and some of us have even become pretty good at disconnecting our daily lives from the truth of who we are as the soul.

If this is you, you're not alone. I've been just as guilty of the tendency to disconnect as you are—maybe even more because I knew what my gifts were and what I was here to do but I still spent years running from it in order to be normal and fit in. No matter how many times the universe gave me a reference point of my purpose—from going into a state of constant bliss in my early 20s for a year and a half to having a near death experience at 29— I didn't listen.

I wanted to be in charge. I wanted to determine what my life would look like. I didn't know how it would look or what people would think if I fully committed to doing what I knew I was here to do and who I was meant to be.

I am—like you—here to fulfill my soul assignment. A task that will frighten you like no other and free you to become the person you're meant to be.

You are meant to outgrow the current version of yourself. Holding back from your soul assignment to stay the same familiar version of yourself for your friends, family, or career all while "doing the work" to manifest your next level doesn't work. It can't work.

It's not your job to make everyone comfortable with the assignment on your soul. It's time to step into the truest and highest version of yourself and create from that.

But how, is the question I get asked most frequently. How do I find my soul assignment and what I'm here to do?

My answer is always the same. It's found in the three priorities of your soul. Your soul priority is to:

1. Remember who you are as a soul.

2. Live your soul assignment by activating and healing your Four Soul Archetypes.

3. Create from your soul something the world has never seen.

The first part of this book—my own personal journey between lifetimes was to help you remember who you are. I shared it because it's not only my story, it's yours too. Although there are variations in the details, your soul went through a similar journey. Now it's time to remember who you are. Go back and help people.

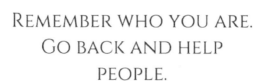

REMEMBER WHO YOU ARE.
GO BACK AND HELP
PEOPLE.

Chapter 8

Where Did the Four Soul Archetypes

Come From?

After my near-death experience, I was never the same. I went from being a 129-pound avid rock climber who had scaled 415,798 feet of vertical rock walls to 200 pounds crawling on the floor. From running my own practice to being unable to turn a doorknob. I had suffered both a near death experience from the accident and had unknowingly contracted Lyme disease three weeks prior to that accident. By the time my doctor diagnosed me with 3rd stage Lyme disease three-and-a-half years later I had suffered so much memory loss there wasn't enough left of me to go back to my old life.

I spent a decade chasing after the woman I knew myself to be. I had received something sacred during the download in my near-death experience but for years felt like I couldn't access it. It was as if I'd been given a box without the ability to open what was inside until one August morning 17 years later it all came rushing through. I had made a full recovery and the Universe decided it was time to open the higher teachings and birth The Four Soul Archetypes into the world.

Chapter 9

Introduction to The Four Soul

Archetypes

Let's reacquaint you with your Soul Archetypes. I wrote "reacquaint" because you've been using these archetypes everyday of your entire life—you just didn't realize they were part of you. Whether you used them in kindness or criticism—you've used them.

There are five truths of your Soul Archetypes:

1.   Everyone   has   Four   Soul Archetypes: The   Expander   Archetype, Connector Archetype, Reflector Archetype, and the Creator Archetype.

2.   Each of the Four Soul Archetypes works on a micro level inside of you and a macro level between all people on Earth and in the Universe.

3.   Each Soul Archetype can be expressed independently but is more effective in partnership.

4.   The Four Soul Archetypes can be expressed on a high level of consciousness or a low level of consciousness.

5.   Your Soul Archetypes remind you of who you are—all the time—whether you're unaware that you're displaying them or are conscious in expressing them.

The Four Soul Archetypes are the bridge from your soul to your daily life. They expand out from within you into the world and contract back into you for you. The path out of an old version of yourself is through your own Soul Archetypes.

When you activate your Soul Archetypes, you grow and often outgrow your current life situation and step into the life you desire. You are meant to express all four of your Soul Archetypes, but you may not have all four activated.

Planted by the divine creator for us to nourish and grow for ourselves, each other, and the planet, one Soul Archetype can activate the other Soul Archetypes. They work together and function at the level of consciousness a person is at. Using them to raise your vibration or help another person will raise your consciousness and using them to hurt others or the planet will lower your consciousness.

The Four Soul Archetypes help you expand into your true self, the highest version of yourself to create what your soul is here to create.

They help you reflect on your path to your own potential. To see what needs healing within you, what's stopping you from going all in on your soul assignment and where you need a shift of perspective.

When you activate and heal all Four Soul Archetypes—you activate and unapologetically live your soul assignment. Your biggest issue isn't that you're not gifted enough or clear enough—it's that you're acting too human. When you begin seeing life through the lens of your soul instead of the limited human mind it's much easier to connect to your soul's work. Your Four Soul Archetypes are the door to a new and higher conscious way of working and living.

YOUR BIGGEST ISSUE
ISN'T THAT YOU'RE NOT
GIFTED ENOUGH OR
CLEAR ENOUGH—IT'S
THAT YOU'RE ACTING
TOO HUMAN.

Chapter 10

The Reflector Archetype

When the Reflector Archetype is healed and activated, they naturally:

1. Reflect the truth of who you are as the soul. They see the truth behind situations and conversations.

2. Reflector Archetypes see the highest potential in others. They see your soul's potential and are happy to share it with you. They see everyone else perfectly clear but often can't see their own genius.

3. They want to help people reach their potential and often choose careers that allow them to do that.

4. They love reflecting the truest image of people who can't see themselves clearly. They can shift someone's limited perspective effortlessly—like holding up a mirror for another to see what they hadn't seen before. Reflector Archetypes are the mirror in which we can see both what we hope to see and what we're avoiding.

5. They see the best in people. They see the soul not the human standing before them. They tend to miss or overlook bad qualities because they are so easily able to feel the soul. The real person behind any bad behavior.

The Reflector Archetype wounds: When your Reflector Archetype is wounded you tend to see everyone else as more qualified, gifted and sometimes even more deserving than you are— even when you're the most gifted person in the room. An activated Reflector Archetype allows you to see others clearly, but the wound is preventing you from seeing yourself clearly. You have a deep sense of your gift which creates an internal conflict between your false belief that others are more gifted than you are and your internal knowing that you are here to help change the world through your gifts.

5 signs your Reflector Archetype is wounded

1. You're in overserving mode. Your Expander, Reflector and Connector Archetypes are on overdrive. You have a tendency to help others expand into more of who they're meant to be, make money

doing what they love and even shine your magical Reflector mirror at them so they can see their own unique gifts—for free. Why? Likely it's an unconscious hope that once you help them get to where they're going, they'll turn back and reflect the truth of you are so you can finally see yourself clearly.

2. You're battling a nearly constant internal conflict of knowing you're gifted but not feeling worthy of using it to earn your living.

3. You see others who are less gifted and experienced than you are becoming successful but don't believe anyone will pay you for your services.

4. You often see or know what the solution to a problem is before anyone else but you keep quiet.

5. You've had or currently have issues with toxic or abusive people.

REFLECTOR ARCHETYPES
ARE HERE TO HELP US
ACTIVATE OUR OWN
SOUL POTENTIAL.

Soul Assignment: When a Reflector Archetype is healed and activated, they see themselves clearly. They stop hiding and downplaying their gifts. Reflector Archetypes are here to help us activate our own soul potential. They see the individual's potential and our global potential and are not afraid to tell people what needs to happen for the outcome we desire.

Client Example: Mary was successful in her career and had the ability to know what her clients needed before they did. Despite her gifts she suffered so much trauma as a child from abuse to homelessness that she couldn't see her own genius. Through our sessions she was able to heal her Reflector Archetype wound, see herself clearly and accept her gifts. She went on to open her own soul aligned business using her Four Soul Archetypes and earns millions of dollars a year doing what she loves now.

Questions and Notes

How are you using your Reflector Archetype in your personal and professional life?

Questions and Notes

What signs (if any) do you notice that your Reflector Archetype may be wounded?

Chapter 11

The Expander Archetype

Here is what you need to know about the Expander Archetype:

1. Expander Archetypes love nothing more than shining their brightest light on the gifts and talents of other Soul Archetypes. They love helping others into the spotlight—a spotlight they probably provided with the help of their Connector Archetype friends.

2. They see and feel the gifts in people, businesses and even situations. Nothing good gets past them without them taking notice.

They get lit up when they discover someone or something that can change the world if given the chance. They see and shine their light on the gifted world changers so the world can see them too.

3. Expander Archetypes help others expand into a greater version of themselves. It's not uncommon that someone with a gift or message to the world can feel too small to carry their own gift or message. Expander Archetypes help those who are meant for more to become the most expansive version of themselves so that they can stand in the spotlight and allow the world to see their gifts, talents, and messages.

4. Expander Archetypes are brilliant at expanding others but usually have trouble expanding themselves.

They need the other Soul Archetypes to push them out of their own comfort zone. Usually, a Reflector Archetype can see and express to an Expander Archetype their own genius in a way that feels aligned and authentic.

5. Expander Archetypes are typically selfless because they're focused on helping those around them expand into who they're meant to be—they aren't in it for themselves. The satisfaction of helping others into the spotlight or expanding into the greatest version of themselves is enough for them.

The Expander Archetype Wounds: If you have an Expander Archetype wound you tend to put everyone else in the spotlight while avoiding it yourself. The interesting thing is, because you're so busy shining your light on everyone around you it often goes unnoticed that you're actually avoiding it yourself.

5 signs your Expander Archetype is wounded.

1. You have a fear of what your family, friends, and community will think of you if you stepped into your full potential and purpose—publicly.

2. You keep busy encouraging and expanding the people around you while purposely avoiding the spotlight yourself. You may even avoid the spotlight by downplaying your appearance.

3. You actually believe you're not meant to be the main attraction because you're so good at spotlighting others. But you can't set an example or pave the way by staying a secret—even though you've tried.

4. You feel conflicted because you're a natural born leader who leads by expanding your team, clients, and company without the need for attention—yet you feel the massive assignment on your soul calling you to do something much bigger.

5. You've self-sabotaged opportunities for real expansion and growth. This type of self-sabotage is usually deep and hidden right under your nose. I've had several clients who were so afraid to step into their full purpose and potential because of how massive it felt that they created one or several situations in their life to hold themselves back. This sometimes showed up as an unhealthy relationship they felt stuck in, their company or clients being totally dependent on them so they couldn't move on, or sometimes they created a life that was so busy they never had the time for their own purpose.

WHEN EXPANDER
ARCHETYPES EXPAND
INTO THE HIGHEST
VERSION OF THEMSELVES
FIRST, THEY CREATE A
PATH FOR OTHERS TO
FOLLOW.

Soul Assignment: Expander Archetypes are here to help us into the higher ages by shining their light onto the souls here to usher in a new and higher conscious way of living and doing business. When they are activated and healed, they quickly expand into the highest version of themselves first—then create a path for others to follow. They are natural leaders and make some of the best leaders because they are so selfless.

Client Example: Stephanie Lynn Salic was a natural born leader working as a project manager at a leading Financial Technology company when we met at a retreat I spoke at. As I worked with her, I was struck by her unusual soul assignment: To usher in a new and higher conscious age of corporate leadership. Only Stephanie's Expander Archetype was blocked from some of her past childhood traumas. While she had done quite a bit of healing before we met, once we healed her Expander wound, she was able to soar to even higher levels of leadership within her company and the world. She became a best-selling author, high conscious mentor and is a sought-after speaker. She continues to climb the corporate ladder since my work with her. Stephanie lives by her Four Soul Archetypes creating and bringing high conscious leadership programs to the world.

Questions and Notes

How are you using your Expander Archetype in your personal and professional life?

Questions and Notes

What signs (if any) do you notice that your Expander Archetype may be wounded?

Chapter 12

The Connector Archetype

The Connector Archetype is what's pulling you to earn your income through your soul assignment and has the following attributes and qualities:

1. Connector Archetypes have a vast network of contacts. The right people come into their lives almost effortlessly.

2. They always feel inspired and happy when they get to make a connection that wouldn't happen without their help. They intuitively know who needs to meet to create opportunities or an impact and they seem to already know

everyone who should be involved. They have an unlimited ability to connect people to people, companies to companies, people to products or services and opportunities to impact.

3. Connector Archetypes lead people and businesses to their potential each day that then activates those around them to create, expand or reflect something for themselves, others or the planet.

4. They love helping connect the world changers to their own network. Connector Archetypes are often activated by the latent potential around them.

5. They serve as a bridge to bring ideas and creation to the world and are geniuses at monetizing it.

The Connector Archetype Wounds: The Connector Archetype wounds are sneaky because you think you're helping people—but mostly you're undercharging or working for free.

Take a good look at your life or business. Are you making your coach, clients, manager or friends a lot of money but not bringing in much for yourself?

Does the idea of making 5 or even 6 figures a month doing what your soul is here to do make you feel uncomfortable?

Have you ever felt like you shouldn't charge for what you can do because you're gifted?

Your Connector Archetype loves to make money, new connections and is here to change the world—but when it's wounded you tend to let others gain from your abilities and gifts without gaining from them yourself.

5 signs your Connector Archetype is wounded.

1. You easily help other people or businesses make money and rise to popularity, but you are not able to do the same for yourself.

2. You refer to other people or businesses but don't get many referrals back.

3. At least some of your self-worth is tied to other successful people you know.

4. You feel it's only ok to make a lot of money as long as you give it away or do something good with it.

5. You pass on opportunities by finding a fault in the opportunity or in yourself.

CONNECTOR
ARCHETYPES SERVE AS A
BRIDGE TO BRING IDEAS
AND CREATION TO THE
WORLD AND ARE
GENIUSES AT
MONETIZING IT.

Soul Assignment: On the deepest level the Connector Archetypes help connect people to their own soul and can connect soul concepts to city or global action. When they are healed and activated Connector Archetypes tend to effortlessly earn their income through the assignment on their soul.

Client Example: Mea, a mother of 2 came to me with deep feelings of unworthiness around what she knew she was meant to do. When she was able to heal her Connector Archetype wound in my Highertherapy™ sessions her Connector Archetype was activated on a higher level. Mea realized she already had in place the people and resources needed to move forward with her soul assignment. She went on to open a successful nonprofit organization dedicated to helping foster and adopted kids throughout her city.

Questions and Notes

How are you using your Connector Archetype in your personal and professional life?

Questions and Notes

What signs (if any) do you notice that your Connector Archetype may be wounded?

Chapter 13

The Creator Archetype

The Creator Archetype is the most precious Soul Archetype because you are here to create from the potential in your soul the most expansive version of yourself for you, for us and the planet.

The Creator Archetype helps bring something new into the world. A new idea, tech, art, music, thought, book or something we've never seen before. When your Creator Archetype is healed and activated you become limitless in your potential and possibilities of bringing to life something the world has never seen.

The Creator Archetype:

1. Creator Archetypes are creating all the time. There is no off switch. They can't stop all the new ideas, thoughts, concepts from coming through them.

2. They are often on a constant overload of new creations and the world around them has no idea this is going on with them. The number of creative ideas downloading into them would overload other Soul Archetypes but to the Creator Archetype it feels normal, even comforting.

3. Creator Archetypes only express a fraction of the ideas they receive. They produce even less than they express. They often feel the world isn't ready for their creations.

4. Creator Archetypes often work best alone. They need their space for the downloads to come through.

Each Creator Archetype has their own process of getting into alignment with what's coming through to them. There's no right way to do it, only their way.

5. Creator Archetypes are private people. They have a world of their own. Unless they have Reflector, Expander and Connector Archetypes in their life to help show them and others their genius they usually won't share their work to the masses.

6. Creator Archetypes are sometimes the least supported and most necessary Soul Archetype. The world relies on them for new ideas, tech, music, art, books, science and innovation but they are often the last to receive support.

The Creator Archetype Wounds: You're hiding from yourself and the world—and you're good at it. You're very likely the only one who knows exactly how talented you are but as long as you feel unsupported and overwhelmed, we'll never see what you're here to create. A fact that simultaneously bothers you and relieves you.

5 signs your Creator Archetype is wounded:

1. You feel like you don't really fit in here. The truth is you don't. You're here to bring in something the world hasn't seen before, so it takes someone extremely unique to do that.

2. You hide from anyone who may discover how talented you are.

3. You're not letting your ideas and creations out of your head and into the world. You may even tell yourself it's because you have too many and can't decide which idea to

share first—but the truth is this is a stalling tactic to keep hiding your brilliance from the world.

4. You aren't charging at all or enough for your creations and ideas.

5. You have trouble feeling like your creative projects are finished.

CREATOR ARCHETYPES,
YOU AREN'T HERE TO DO
EVERYONE ELSE'S JOB—
YOU'RE HERE TO DO
WHAT NO ONE ELSE CAN
DO.

Soul Assignment: Creator Archetypes are meant to be supported by high conscious Reflector, Connector, and Expander Archetypes. When they are healed and activated, they can do what the other archetypes can't do: Create something out of thin air that can give humanity what it needs to move into the higher ages. Creator Archetypes, you aren't here to do everyone else's job—you're here to do what no one else can do.

Client Example: When my client's mother reached out to me her daughter Nina had been home for 18 months after serving six years in prison. In those 18 months she hadn't left her bedroom. Prior to prison she was a talented honors student at a top college in New York. When we healed her Creator Archetype wound in my Highertherapy™ session she was able to understand her deeper life and soul's purpose. She came out of her room for the first time in 18 months and began creating the most beautiful and powerful art from her soul. She found her true desire and passion and went on to study at one of the most prestigious visual effects schools in the country.

Questions and Notes

How are you using your Creator Archetype in your personal and professional life?

Questions and Notes

What signs (if any) do you notice that your Creator Archetype may be wounded?

Chapter 14

The Unhealed Soul Archetype

Interactions with an unhealed Soul Archetype can be challenging. The Four Soul Archetypes are powerful and while they hold the potential to live aligned with the Soul, they can be misused. When they are misused, it hurts deep.

For example, an unhealed Reflector Archetype is just as capable of using their abilities as a healed Reflector Archetype. They can see you, but have the ability to twist the beautiful truth of who you are into something ugly and effortlessly make you believe their version of you. Each of the Four Soul Archetypes can be used for the greatest good or to intentionally hurt someone.

When one of your Four Soul Archetypes is wounded by an unhealed Soul Archetype, that wound can hold you back from living and expanding into your greatest potential. Unhealed Soul Archetypes tend toward more toxic behavior; the wounded Soul Archetypes tend to have trouble with limiting beliefs about who they are and what they're truly capable of.

Both are in need of healing and once healing is engaged, they each hold the potential to create the most magnificent lives.

Chapter 15

Soul Archetypes in The Work Place

No matter where you work, no matter what your chosen career path is your Soul Archetypes are within you and everyone around you. When you align with your Four Soul Archetypes in your work you feel happiest, in flow and are the most financially abundant.

I believe the reason many work environments have become increasingly stressful is because the people working there are not working from their souls. The Four Soul Archetypes are the bridge to connect your everyday life with your soul assignment.

While you have all Four Soul Archetypes, they may not all be activated or healed. Each Soul Archetype has a career they excel at. You always want to be working from your most activated and healed Soul Archetypes so you can live your purpose and create limitless abundance in all areas of your life.

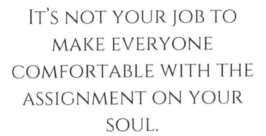

IT'S NOT YOUR JOB TO
MAKE EVERYONE
COMFORTABLE WITH THE
ASSIGNMENT ON YOUR
SOUL.

Chapter 16

The Activation

As you intentionally activate your Soul Archetypes, your vibratory and spiritual consciousness will awaken and elevate to higher levels. Activating your Soul Archetypes can be as simple as being present with them and looking for opportunities to use them in your daily life to help others or yourself.

You are made for more and it's your own soul calling out asking you to expand into the highest and truest version of yourself. Activate your Soul Archetypes and answer your soul's call.

Thank you for being on this journey with me. I have enjoyed our time together. For your free Soul Archetype Assessment visit me at:

www.soulpriority.com

Acknowledgements

I acknowledge the extraordinary people whose gifts touched my soul and this book.

To my husband Chris Frederick, thank you for your endless strength, eternal love, faith and for always believing in me. Thank you for finding me again—you have great timing.

To my editor and friend Mary L. Holden for being a guardian angel for this book. Your insights and visions are from the highest realms, and I couldn't have gotten here without your perseverance and grace.

To Lisa Tener, thank you for sharing your Harvard writing wisdom, your meticulous notes, suggestions, and corrections.

To Steph Zahalka, book cover designer, brand consultant and graphic artist—

thank you for cosmically downloading and drawing The Four Soul Archetypes. Thank you for seeing what I needed and creating it.

To the incomparable Natasha Leigh Bray, thank you for seeing my soul.

To Amanda and Marcus Papay, thank you for generously sharing such a magical piece of land to work, think and receive my downloads.

To Swami Padmananda for encouraging me to finish this book and telling me what my soul needed to hear.

To the late Roy Eugene Davis, my time with you was some of the most precious in this life. Thank you, you were right. I did know when this book was ready.

To my family, friends, chosen family and clients thank you for your love, support and years of excitement during the writing of this book.

A special thank you to my readers. You aren't here by accident, and I'm honored that you spent time reading my book. Thank you for participating with me on this book's journey.

Made in United States
Troutdale, OR
12/10/2023

15622925R00080